I0440998

The Awesome Power of 'Respect'!

Solving Problems in Race Relations

By

Rodney R Letchworth

Lieutenant Colonel

USMC Retired

The Awesome Power of Respect

Table of Contents

Chapter One

The B. C. Long Philosophy

I was raised in Tallahassee, FL, in the heart of the 'Deep Segregated South'. I never knew a black person as a person. I only knew them as lazy, ignorant individuals who were always the brunt of derogatory jokes!

It was the Segregated South! There was no alternative view for a young white boy! During my Marine Corps career, up to the events described herein, I also had little opportunity to get to know any black Marines.

After a relatively successful Marine Corps career in which I had been selected 'Recruit of the Year' in 1957; scored the highest score that had ever been recorded by a Naval Aviation Cadet at the U.S Naval School Preflight in 1958; flown three years in the "Blacksheep Squadron", VMA-214 in 1962 as a Nuclear Weapons Delivery Pilot; flown 289 Combat Mission in Vietnam 1968 in the A4 Skyhawk; graduated from the U. S. Naval Postgraduate School in Monterey, CA.1972; instructed 2 years with the "Marine Corp Top Gun School", a euphemism for MAAWTU-PAC (Marine Advanced Air Weapons Training Unit-Pacific); I received a very strange set of orders!

These orders stated that I <u>would</u> attend a "Human Relations Course" for 3 weeks. After completing that school I <u>would</u> report to The Commanding General of The First Marine Aircraft Wing; Iwakuni, Japan for duty as the, "First Marine Aircraft Wing, Human Affairs Officer".

I found out, when I arrived at the school, that the Marine Corp was having a "Serious Race Relations Problem" but had been advised by academic professionals to call it a "<u>Human Relations Problem</u>", not a Race Relations Problem.

This assignment was the "Pivotal Experience of my life! I learned more about people in that one year and 3 weeks than I had learned during all my previous 37 years of being alive on this planet!

The first thing I learned was that Black People are really People! I mean really people just like me! I had never been around enough black people to get to know any of them as a person!

At our "Human Relations School" I met a black Marine Captain. His name was B.C. Long. I very quickly realized that B.C. was at least as intelligent as I am, and probably had more brainpower than I had. He was very well educated, personable, humorous, pleasant, and easy to talk to.

It was an eye opener for me to meet a real black person and be able to communicate with him as a person! We quickly became the best of friends! I felt so at ease with B.C. that I was comfortable disclosing to him my previous prejudiced background. He understood and never seemed to be offended.

I learned more from B.C. Long about people and people relations than I had learned during my entire previous life. We were able to discuss the issues of Race Relations frankly and without any worry that we might not understand each other!

The school we were attending was a course prepared by a group of professors from a prominent University, which shall be nameless. They wanted to point out how a military organization was much like a family. Both have members who are dependent on each other for success and survival.

The course was prepared so that one individual from each squadron in an Air Wings would be sent to Air Wing Headquarters; receive a course of instructions in "Human Relations"; and then go back to his Squadron and teach other Marines there how to successfully interact with each other as a family.

The University Professionals had prepared this course of instructions, along with a slide show for visual effects.

The <u>Very First Slide</u> portrayed a family of "BABOONS"! The narrative for the slide was a description of how all the members in a family of Baboons stick together and defend each other to the <u>death</u> when, any member of the family is threatened by a Leopard or any other predator.

The implication was that all members of a Squadron should consider themselves a family and be prepared to defend each other from outside threats.

After the class I asked B. C., "What do you think of this approach?" He laughed! "Obviously none of these professors are from the South" he said. "Otherwise they would have known that the word 'Baboon' is <u>the</u> worst 'Racial Slur' that can be used to describe a Black Person!"

After class, B.C. and I spent many hours discussing the problems involved in Race Relations. It was so refreshing to have an intelligent conversation with such an intelligent person about a problem so fraught with pitfalls.

One day I asked B.C. "What do Black People <u>really want</u>?" I have never forgotten his answer. He only said one word. He said "Respect"! I wanted more information, but he only had the one word – "Respect".

What I finally got from our conversation was that Black Marines only wanted to be respected for the work they were performing as Marines. They wanted to think that their superiors were aware of their contributions to the success of the organization. They would be satisfied and happy to have their superiors occasionally recognize their efforts! That recognition could be as simple as saying "Good Morning, Marine!", and stressing the word 'Marine'! This would be a way of showing Respect! That is the only thing Black Marines want – Respect'! Captain Long had a keen perception, and a remarkable knowledge. It was from him I learned the 'Awesome Power of Respect'.

Captain Long kept repeating that Black Marines do **not** want any 'Special Treatment' or 'Special Favors'. They only want 'Equal Respect' for the job they are doing. After many hours of brainstorming we came up with a plan. The underlying principles of the plan was simple.

1. Race Relations can never be improved from the Bottom Up! They can only be improved from the top down. Any attempt by a Junior Black Marine to improve relations, will always appear to any Senior White Marine to be an act of "kissing ass" or "sucking up" in an attempt to get special treatment. It is incumbent therefore upon the Senior White Marine to initiate all attempts to improve race relations.

2. If Step 1 is successful there will not be any need for a step 2. If it is not successful, forget it, you won't ever get there!!

Chapter Two

The Iwakuni Experiment

I left for Iwakuni, Japan with fear and trembling, but with a fire in my soul! I was determined I would not be bullied by the Brass. I was also aware of the mindset of most Senior White Officers in the Marine Corps at that time.

I knew that the vast majority of these men were from the South and probably just as prejudiced as I had been before meeting Captain B.C. Long. This was a decision I struggled with long and hard!

The pros and cons were simple: I could butt my head against this brick wall; try everything I could to improve life for Black Marines, and thus improve Race Relations. Or I could punt: (kiss ass and pretend to be interested in helping, all the while avoiding any appearance to the Brass that I was the least bit interested in improving the lives of Black Marines, or improving Race Relations in the Marine Corps.)

My Decision was made and I felt good about it! I decided that even though my hopes of ever making General Officer in the U.S. Marine Corps would probably be over, I would not shrink from what I felt was my duty as a human being!

I knew that the best I could ever hope for after this assignment would be a 20 year Marine Corps career! And then it would be over for me! (Retirement).

I knew I could be Court Marshalled and 'Cashiered Out' immediately! However I also knew that I would never be able to look at myself in the mirror again if I let Captain B.C. Long down!

I thought long and hard about a strategy which would be effective. I knew that any plan I came up with had to be concealed from the brass in order to be effective.

I could not confide in anyone or expect anyone to help me – not even my own staff with whom I had attended Human Relations School. I didn't know how I would do it, but I knew what I wanted to accomplish and actually got excited as I looked for opportunities to make it happen.

When I arrived in Iwakuni, Japan, I checked in and found that I would be assigned to work for a Lieutenant Colonel, (who shall be nameless to protect the guilty!). He was a deputy to the G1 (Personnel) of the Air Wing. My staff, all classmates from 'Human Relations School', had arrived before me and had set up an office for me. All these good guys were Lieutenants and all White Men.

I had been a Major for 3 years and so I had a little seniority which I used to advantage occasionally.

Everything was as I had suspected and so I knew what my boss had been told by the Commanding General, Major General Anonymous.   General Anonymous was a "Good Ole Boy" from Virginia and thoroughly possessed by all the prejudices of a Southern Gentlemen.

I was to complete my assignment from the Commandant of The Marine Corps as quickly as possible. However I was warned that none of my activities could interfer with any of his Squadron Commanders, or their operational assignments!   After all, many of these Marines were fighting a war in Vietnam!

My immediate senior officer, Lt Col Noname, did not want to know what I was doing or where I was going, or when I planned to return. I <u>was</u> notified however, that under no circumstance would I be going into Country (into Vietnam). At that time, we had two Air Groups and 12 Squadrons in Vietnam heavily engaged in Combat Operations. The Commandant of the Marine Corps had commanded that All Marines, including Officers, had to receive the required Human Relations Training Course. Altogether my people had to teach more than 2000 Marines a course in "Human Relations". The reason for my "Travel Restrictions" was because I had worked in the MAWTU Pac, 'Top Gun' Unit, and had been required to use Highly Classified Information. This information could possibly have been "compromised", had I been captured while in South Vietnam teaching "Human Relations".

I studied my situation carefully and came up with a plan. The first thing I did was to have all the pictures of baboons removed from our literature and <u>burned</u>!

The next thing I did was tell my boss, LtCol. Noname that I did not recommend having every squadron in the Air Wing send one man to Iwakuni for a three week Human Relations course. The time required to identify these instructors; transport them to Japan; train them and then return them to their squadron would disrupt combat operation unnecessarily.

This was the procedure recommended by the Baboons at the College of Experts! They wanted a person who was a "member of the family" to take the message of "Family Unity" back to each Squadron. I knew this would never work! The "messengers" would have been laughed out of the room.

My recommended source for Human Relations Instructors, was to find Marines currently located at Iwakuni. I suggested to my boss that we could significantly reduce any chance of interfering with 'Combat' operations, if we selected instructors from the men serving in Wing Headquarters and local Squadrons in Iwakuni. We could give them a crash course in "Human Affairs" and then send these men to each Squadron in the Air Wing, (including those fighting in

Combat in Vietnam). Using this approach we would complete the operation in a fraction of the time and with a minimum of disruptions to Combat Operations.

My boss bought the idea and presented it to the General as if it were his own. The General approved the plan and I got busy. I knew that 'no one could know' what I was doing, or they would see to it that I was stopped!

To really make my plan work, I needed some Black Marines who could speak effectively and convincingly in public! These men were hard to find in the Marine Corps at that time! Black People had been taught, especially in the South, that subservience was required for survival. I knew from my childhood experience that Black People had been taught to never speak in the presence of a White person unless they had been spoken to first.

I knew, however, that there were Black Marines at Iwakuni at that time who did have the skills I needed, and I knew where to find them!

Iwakuni had been one of the Bases where a Race Riot had occurred. It was one of those Riots which had precipitated the Commandant's action! Upon learning of the Riots the Commandant had immediately commissioned the College of Expert to prepare a course of instruction in Human Relations. He then commanded that ALL Marines attend a Required Course in Human

Relations. The riot at Iwakuni was one of the more serious riots! One White Marine had lost an eye when an angry Black Marine had gouged it out with a Coke bottle! Some of the Black Marines who had organized and led the Race Riot were still in the Iwakuni Brig. Most of them, however, had recently been released from confinement. Yes, I knew where I could find my 'Human Relations Instructors'! If only I could persuade these Black Marines to help me!

First I went to the Air Wing G2 (Intelligence Officer). I knew he had the names of the perpetrators. It wasn't easy to get these names! I had to convince the Intelligence Officer that I was working for and speaking for the Wing Commander, Major General Anonymous. The G2 officer finally, reluctantly, agreed, and gave me the names.

Then the <u>really hard work </u>began – persuading the Race Riot Perpetrators, for whom I was trying to make life easier; that I needed their public speaking ability to make the plan work. I could not let anyone know what I was up to! By word of mouth I arranged to meet each of these Black Marines; separately on different days; in one of the Beer Joints in a remote section of Iwakuni. I wore only civilian clothing, and tried to avoid attracting any attention!

At each meeting I talked my head off trying to convince these men that I was trying to help them! I said, "Man I know you're mad! What I want to know is 'Do you want to change things, or just keep on complaining? I'm here to try and change things! I want to make life easier for all you Black Marines! I'm willing to risk my career in the Marine Corp in order to make things better for you! I love my Marine Corps; but I know that what you guys are living with is <u>wrong</u>! Will you help me? I need <u>your</u> help, or my plan won't work! <u>Will you help me?</u>

I didn't find anyone brave enough to help; until I asked the third man. He agreed, but he warned me that if it didn't work, he would find me and get even! He knew that this could have been a trap!

After I recruited the first one, all the rest were easier: the first ones to accept my offer went back and convinced the earlier ones that I was on the level. They also knew that I was <u>putting my career</u> on the line <u>to help them</u>! We became very good friends, the lot of us! I knew that they had started the riot because they had 'just had enough!'

Putting my plan into place required the utmost secrecy! Even my classmates from Human Relations School in California could not know what I was doing. When we started training Human Relations Instructors at Iwakuni, they were <u>the</u> men I had met with in the bars and persuaded to join us. I requested these men by name through normal channels so none of the hardline,

Senior Officers ever suspected. Even my own subordinates; classmates from our California Human Relations School; never suspected!

The Plan Worked! We trained the men I had recruited, plus a few other men we had recruited from Squadrons there at Iwakuni. We then formed these trained Instructors into teams and began deploying the teams to all the Squadrons in the Air Wing. We started with the Squadrons which were engaged in Combat in Vietnam.

When they arrived at each Squadron, they briefed the Squadron Commander on the plan. The plan called for the Squadron to "Stand Down" - cease all operations - for one day. During that day the members of the Squadron were required to meet in designated places and listen to our "teachers" tell them what each Marine would be required to do every day; from that day on; until they rotated home after completing their tour of duty in the First Marine Air Wing!

****

Here is the course which I prepared:
For each class I had my Instructors read the following statement:

"This is the expressed command of:
Brigadier General Anonymous,
Command General,
First Marine Air Wing":

> "1) Each time a <u>Senior White Officer</u> encounters a <u>Junior Black Marine</u> who is rendering a Hand Salute; that Officer <u>will</u> return the salute with these words … 'Good Morning MARINE', <u>emphasizing </u>the word 'MARINE' because it shows 'RESPECT!
>
> 2) - Each time a <u>Senior White</u> Enlisted Marine encounters a <u>Junior Black </u>Marine he will say these words … 'Good Morning MARINE!', <u>emphasizing</u> the word 'MARINE' because it shows 'RESPECT'."

After reading the above Quote from Major General Anonymous, each instructor was required to break out the Course from the College of Experts (minus the Baboon pictures); and talk for two hours about how a family must fight to defend each other when any danger threatens any member of the family! After this the group would discuss how this "Family" concept related to a Squadron's operations. When the discussion ended, my Instructor would close his meeting with the following instructions:

This is the expressed command of:
Brigadier General Anonymous,
Commanding General,
First Marine Air Wing:

> "1) – Each time a <u>Senior White</u> Officer encounters a <u>Junior Black</u> Marine who is rendering a Hand Salute; that Officer <u>will</u> return the salute with these words … 'Good Morning MARINE', <u>emphasizing</u> the word 'MARINE' because it shows 'RESPECT!'
> 2) - Each time a <u>Senior White</u> Enlisted Marine encounters a <u>Junior Black</u> Marine he will say these words … 'Good Morning MARINE!', <u>emphasizing</u> the word 'MARINE' because it shows 'RESPECT'."

That was the SUM TOTAL of our "Human Relations Course!"

When I arrived at Iwakuni, there had been an average of 60 "Racial Incidents" per month (two Racial Incident per day) for the preceding 10 months; including the Two Major Race Riots! All these incidents had been reported to the Secretary of Defense as required.

Three months after I arrived and my people had finished teaching this course of instruction to 2000+ members of the First Marine Air Wing; the racial incidents had been REDUCED DRAMATICALLY!: They had dropped from <u>60 per month to Zero</u> !

There was not one single Racial Incident during the remaining nine months of my tour.

Captain B. C. Long was absolutely correct! "The <u>Power of Respect is Awesome</u>"! It could not have been demonstrated more dramatically! It was a rotten shame that I could not have shared this secret at that time with the WORLD!

The sudden change in Race Relations in the First Marine Air Wing caught the sharp eye of a young analyst at the Pentagon. Shortly thereafter, he showed up at my door wanting to know how I had done it! I promised to tell him, but not before I had sworn him to secrecy.

After I had explained everything to him, he wanted to meet my Instructors. I introduced him and they all confirmed what I had told him. He returned to Washington and reported his findings to the Secretary of Defense.

Our General Anonymous <u>immediately</u> received a "Letter of Commendation" signed by the Secretary of Defense. The General later received a 'Legion of Merit' Medal in which the Citation included "...for his achievements in the field of 'Human Affairs'. "

After it was over, General Anonymous found out from his Squadron Commanders what I had done. He instructed my boss, LtCol Noname to quietly give me an 'Unsatisfactory Fitness Report' which had to be strong enough to ensure that I would never be promoted again in the Marine Corps! He was afraid to take any stronger action because he was afraid of any adverse publicity which might result.

Fortunately for me, my next assignment was to become the Head of Marine Aviation Studies and Analyses in Washington, D.C. This was an assignment I had been educated for at the Naval Postgraduate School, Monterey, California.

I had no trouble getting the "Unsatisfactory Fitness Report" removed from my official records. I even got it removed before the Lieutenant Colonel Promotion Board met. All I needed was the records from the Department of Defense containing the young analyst's report to the Secretary of Defense, and a copy of the resulting SecDef "Letter of Commendation" for Major General Anonymous.

With these records I petitioned the "Board for Correction of Naval Records"! After a hearing where I presented the documents, and explained in detail what I had done, why I had done it, and what the results were; the Board removed the 'Unsatisfactory Fitness Report' from my official records. The Board Members then enthusiastically congratulated me for the accomplishment!

Shortly thereafter I was promoted to Lieutenant Colonel! I served three years as Head of Marine Corps Aviation Studies and Analyses at Marine Headquarters, Washington, D.C. This was followed by the assignment of a lifetime: Commanding Officer of an A4 Skyhawk/Headquarters & Maintenance Squadron. Every Marine Pilot Dreams of becoming a Squadron Commander! After that assignment, I retired. I would love to have reached the rank of General, but I knew it would have been foolish to wait around for it. There were too many Southern Generals still on active duty which would have made it impossible.

In summary, I discovered a new life after meeting Captain Long. I learned the "Awesome Power of 'Respect'." I had always heard that Black People wanted "EQUALITY"! "Equal Rights", "Equal Opportunity", "Equal Education". What I found out from Captain Long was that what they really want more than any of these; they want RESPECT!

It was a remarkable achievement to completely eliminate all serious Race Relations problems in an organization of 2000+ people; scattered over Three Countries, (Japan, Okinawa, and Vietnam) in just three months! I am proud to have been a part of the achievement, but more important to me was the knowledge I gained about how very "POWERFUL" the concept of "RESPECT" really is.

Chapter Three

Leadership Failure Caused by Lack of Respect

In 1975 I was serving as the Head of Marine Corps Aviation Studies and Analyses. My office was in Marine Corps Headquarters, Washington, D.C.

One day I was informed that I had been selected to serve on a Study Group headed by a Brigadier General. The Group had been charged to study the problem and find out why a very large number of Marines had left the Marine Corp before completing their enlistments.

The year before, (1974), thirty four percent (34%) of Marines leaving the Marine Corps had left without an 'Honorable Discharge'!

Whenever Marines leave without finishing their obligated and sworn duty, they receive a 'Less than Honorable Discharge' or in some cases a 'Dishonorable

Discharge'. They then encounter very difficult circumstances back in civilian life. Jobs are hard to find, in fact they are almost impossible to find. Most employers feel that anyone with this history is untrustworthy and undesirable.

Thirty Four Percent of all Marines was an alarmingly high number! It reflected poorly on the reputation of the Corps throughout the Nation after it had been reported in the National Press!

Newspapers were asking for answers! Officers were scrambling! Records were being searched and heads were about to roll! The Commandant was furious that this had happened on his watch! His instructions to those of us on the Study Group was: "Get me some answers NOW!"

The Study Group consisted of one Brigadier General, three Lieutenant Colonels, three Majors, three Captains, and a number of clerical personnel. I was a Major at the time. The General had us all introduce ourselves and tell where we worked and what our backgrounds included. After we finished our introductions, he asked for ideas about how to start the 'study'.

Most of the suggestions offered, indicated that our recruiting standards and qualifications were defective. I made the suggestion that we investigate the quality of leadership in the organizations where most of the unhappy Marines had been serving immediately before being discharged. It seemed to me that a man who is so unhappy that he will take any punishment to get out of the Marine Corps; must be serving under pretty onerous circumstances. This suggestion was <u>not received kindly</u> by the group!

After a few more discussions, we were dismissed with the order to get something before the next meeting. He then gave us the date and time for our next meeting.

At our next meeting, there were several ideas presented and a few specific data points provided. Most of the ideas were aimed at placing the total blame on the 'deserters'. I was the only one who dared to suggest that 'Leadership Failures' might have played a part. Once again we were charged to dig up data to back up our ideas.

Then it was show and tell time. We each had to present data to support our theories. One of the really sharp Captains presented his data to support his theory that we were accepting less than desirable recruits. He produced data which revealed that a very high percentage of those leaving early did not have a High School Diploma. They had been allowed to enlist with only a GED (General Education Development) Certificate. His theory was that someone who quit High School before graduating was more likely to quit the Marine Corps before completing his enlistment.

I thought that the Captain had done some scholarly work, but I also thought that there was more to the problem than this one factor. My research had included a computer search of the personnel files of all Captains, Majors, and Lieutenant Colonels in the Marine Corps. The data I had extracted was the "Leadership" ratings and current assignments of all these officers.

I then grouped the officers into those like me who were located in Washington, and those who were in billets where they were in Command of, and in daily contact with junior Marines. Then I collected the data as to where the young Marines had been assigned when they had decided to leave the Marine Corps early.

It turned out that the officers with the best scores in 'Leadership' were predominately all in Washington pushing paper. Those with the lowest scores in 'Leadership' were out in the Field; actually they were in the Commands where most of the young Marines had been assigned immediately before leaving the Marine Corps. I concluded that these young Marines had endured as much "Dis Respect" as they could take, and wanted out no matter what it cost!

I had started out my Marine Corps Career as a Recruit at Parris Island, South Carolina. After graduation from Boot Camp, I had been assigned as a Rifle Instructor. I worked in that assignment for two years before going to Flight School. During my time at Parris Island I had witnessed some glaring examples of poor leadership. In other assignments from the Philippians to Okinawa, to Hawaii, to Japan, to Vietnam I had also witnessed some bad scenes. Thus my desire to examine this possible cause of the current crisis in the Marine Corps.

The General in charge of our Study took the findings of our Study Group to the Commandant. The Commandant accepted the Captain's findings as the only cause of the problem: i.e. no High School diploma. He then changed the recruiting requirements to include a High School Diploma. No longer could a young man enter the Marine Corps with only a GED, He must have a High School Diploma!

Our Study Group General came back from the Commandant's Office with the news. The Commandant had issued a press release announcing that the problem had been solved! No longer would the Marine Corps accept a GED education! From then on – all Marine Recruit applicants must have an actual High School Diploma!

After announcing the results of his visit to the Commandant, our General asked me 'privately', to stay after he dismissed the other members. When all had left and we were alone, the General said to me: "The Commandant told me to tell you this personally: 'If 'One Word' of your study results gets into the National News – Your ass is grass!" I said "Yes Sir, My lips are sealed!"

In less than two weeks after the Commandant's Press Release we witnessed a mass exodus of Captains, Majors, and Lieutenant Colonels from Marine Corps Headquarters!

The Problem had been solved immediately! None of the reporters from the National Press ever got a clue about what had actually caused the disgraceful event! If the change in recruiting qualifications had been responsible, the effects would have taken years to produce the results we had seen in just weeks. The troops no longer had to serve under hardline, whip cracking bullies. They were getting real 'Leaders'; Officers who realized the value of positive motivation; Officers who treated all Marines in their command with dignity and RESPECT!

Chapter Four

The Role of Respect in Positive Leadership

'One Example'

After completing 3 years in Washington as Head of Marine Corps Aviation Studies and Analyses, my last assignment in the Marine Corps was the 'Assignment of a Lifetime'! I became Commanding Officer of an A4 Skyhawk Squadron! Actually, my command was Commanding Officer of H&MS 13 (Headquarters and Maintenance Squadron 13). This squadron was a complex collection of responsibilities.

We served Marine Air Group 13 as a combination Administration, Intermediate Level Maintenance Facility and Supply Depot. The Air Group consisted of A4 Skyhawk Squadrons, F4 Phantom Squadrons and an A6 Intruder Squadron.

We also operated a small fleet of TA4 Skyhawk aircraft for use by the MAWTU-PAC (Marine Air Weapons Training Unit Pacific). MAWTU was the Marine Corps' "Top Gun School"! Selected pilots from all Marine Squadrons on the West Coast and throughout the Pacific

Commands were brought to El Toro for a three month course in "Air Combat Maneuvering" (Dogfighting), and other specialized and demanding flight maneuvers. The A4 Skyhawk had performance specifications very similar to the Russian MIG-21. It made a very good bird to engage the Navy's "Top Gun" students at nearby Miramar Naval Air Station (San Diego) in air combat maneuvering. So we considered MAWTU the "Top Gun" School of the Marine Corps.

We also engaged the Air Force and Navy Pilots at Nellis Air Force Base, Las Vegas, Nevada in the annual "Red Flag" competition.

I had this job for only one year – then I retired. Why retire? Well the story goes back a long way.

Before I go back to those days, to explain the background to this decision to retire, let me talk about some of the fun I had as Commanding Officer.

I had started my Marine Corp Career as a Private (E1) at Marine Corps Recruit Training Depot (Boot Camp), Parris Island, S.C. There I began to witness the unusual relationship between Officers and Enlisted People in the Marine Corps.

There is a need in any military organization to maintain "Good Order and Discipline". This is accomplished by establishing a proper relationship between "Leaders" and "Followers". The relationship is accomplished by establishing rules of conduct for Officers and Enlisted Personnel. Rules like "Never Fraternize with your Troops" are frequently misinterpreted to mean "Never get to know your troops, and never let your troops get to know you."

Having started as an enlisted man, I never had this problem. Although I never went out on 'Liberty' with any of my troops, I engaged with them in all the activities I could as their Commanding Officer. This way I had a chance to get to know them as people and not just as employees.

When I became Commanding Officer of a squadron with 600+ enlisted people, I wanted to establish a relationship of trust with each one of My Marines

I started my quest for a reputation of 'Respect' for the men of my command by having a formation with all personnel who were not employed in a critical, "mission-essential" activity. The formation was held in front of my main Hanger/Squadron Headquarters.

When the troops were in place I appeared in front of the Senior Enlisted Man who had organized the formation; and receive his report. When he reported, "All personnel present and accounted for, SIR!" I returned his salute and said "Very well! Take your post!" He took his position in the formation and I commanded,

"Left Face, Forward March." Then I commanded "Double Time, March!" We 'Counted Cadence' as we passed our Air Group Commander's Office. We proceeded to the offices of the Wing Commander, and then to all the other Squadrons on the base. As you can imagine we made quite a lot of noise! By the time we returned to our Hanger after passing all the Hangers and Administrative Buildings counting cadence at the top of our voices, my troops were laughing their heads off! When I called them to a 'Halt', I could just feel the electricity in the air.

After I finally got them quiet I said, "Alright Men, you have nowhere to hide! Everybody on this base knows who <u>you</u> are and who <u>we</u> are! From now on I want you to know that YOU represent H&MS-13! From this day on, you <u>will always</u> go out in a fresh, starched, sharp uniform; with a proper haircut, and a big smile on your face like you're PROUD to be a Marine! Does everyone understand me?" There was such a loud roar it was deafening! I never had a disciplinary problem again.

To maintain the good morale I challenged the Commanding Officer of the squadron next door to a "Physical Fitness Contest". We all had to take the test every 3 months anyway; so why not have a little fun, and promote some competition and comradery?

The other squadron was a Marine Air Base Squadron (MABS). They had many jobs, but one of their primary jobs was "Bomb Humper". They maintained a bomb dump and loaded bombs on each aircraft for every bombing mission. These Marines were strong!

It was ludicrous for me to challenge these guys to a strength test! I knew very well that we probably wouldn't win; but I wanted my men to know that I believed in them!

It was a roaring success! I was first in line for every contest. The men of both squadrons watched as their Commanding Officer and our Commanding Officer (me), started the competition with the 'pull-up, chin-up' event.

The minimum acceptable pull-ups were 3. Their Commanding Officer did 5 pull-ups. I hadn't told anyone, but this was my best event. I did 22 pull-ups! My troops sent up a roar that was heard all the way to Group Headquarters!

Needless to say, their final score was out in orbit compared to ours; but none of that mattered in the least! The only thing that I wanted to happen - did happen. The morale in my squadron was off the page and everyone on the base knew it!

Some months later our Air Group Commander responded to some of my efforts to show my respect for my men by organizing a competition of his own among all the squadrons in our Air Group.

He had put a lot of thought into his contest. He could not involve everyone in the Air Group (about 2500 people) so he created a very ingenious contest!

His contest was a "Relay Race"! The 'Baton' was not a bamboo stick to be handed off from one runner to the next. His "Baton" was a 25 pound inert "Practice Bomb"! Each contestant had to run one lap (1/4 mile) carrying a 25 lb. inert bomb which they would then hand off to the next runner.

Each of our five squadrons provided 13 runners; 8 enlisted men, ranks E1-E8 (Private – Sergeant Major); and then 5 officers, ranks O1-O5 (Second Lieutenant – Lt. Colonel).

The race began with the 5 Privates, one from each squadron, rounding the track carrying their 25 lb. bomb. After completing their Quarter-mile they passed the bomb to their squadron's Private First Class, who then rounded the track and passed the bomb to the Corporal, etc. until the baton (bomb) ended up in the hands of the Squadron Commander for the final lap.

When I received my bomb, the A6 Intruder Squadron's Commanding Officer, my friend Fred, was in the lead about 1/3 lap ahead of me. I knew it would be near impossible, but I knew my men were counting on me so I had no choice – I had to catch Fred! It took a superhuman effort but I passed Fred about 10 feet before we crossed the finish line!

The roar of my crowd for that last 1/4th lap was heard all the way across the Base!

Needless to say I have wonderful memories of this, my final year in the U.S. Marine Corps! It was wonderful to see again that the awesome power of 'Respect' rendered to junior Marines was indeed – 'AWESOME'!

Chapter Five

Using the Awesome Power of 'Respect' to Improve Race Relations

My experience in using the 'Awesome Power of Respect' in the Military, has convinced me that this 'Idea" could be used to dramatically improve 'Race Relations' in the civilian population of the United States of America!

Yes, the Military is a 'Structured Organization' with well-defined levels of authority; much different than our less structured Civilian Society. However, the Principles of 'Organized Equal <u>Respect</u> for Equal <u>Performance</u>' could be used to dramatically reduce Racial Tensions in America.

Most 'Racial Conflicts are caused by the 'Perception of Discrimination', rather than the existence of 'Actual Discrimination'! It is always easier to prevent 'Racial Conflict', than it is to resolve 'Racial Conflict'!

Before discussing 'Methodologies' for preventing Racial Conflicts, it might be constructive to agree on a set of 'Principles' which must be incorporated into all Methodologies selected in order to ensure success.

Principles for Success in Race Relations!

The B. C Long Principles for

Success in Improving Race Relations in <u>any</u> Society!

Principle Number One:

> Race Relations can <u>never be improved from the Bottom Up</u>! They can <u>only be improved from the top down</u>. Any attempt by a Black Member (or any other Minority Member) of a Society to improve relations, will <u>always</u> appear to a White Superior to be an act of "kissing ass" or "sucking up" in an attempt to get <u>special treatment</u>. It is incumbent therefore upon the <u>Senior Member</u> of the Majority Population in any organization to initiate <u>all attempts</u> to improve race relations.

Principle Number Two:

If Principle 1 is successful there will not be any need for Principle 2

If Principle 1 is not successful, forget it! You won't ever get there!

With these two Principles let us seek to find some Methodologies for improving Race Relations in America. These are only my ideas. I know that there are many professional in this Nation who are more qualified than I to develop Methodologies using these Principles. There are many reasons why I believe this. Some reasons are:

First, there are people more intelligent than I am.

Second, there are people more educated than I am.

Third, there are people much younger than I am at 80 years old.

Fourth, there are people who are in positions of power who desperately Need to find solutions for their 'Race Relations Problems'.

Therefore I offer these suggestions:

1. The Senior member of the Majority Race at every level of authority in the Legislative ,Executive, and Administrative Organizations at the National, State, and City, level, including Law Enforcement be REQUIRED BY LAW to publicly "Recognize" the contributions of all minority employees by daily greeting them with a smile and a friendly comment.   This shows "RESPECT" for their contributions to the success of the organization!

2. If this Method fails to improve Race Relations in America – Forget it. We won't ever get there.

Footnote:

I firmly believe that when we have enough members of Black and other Minorities in positions of Political and Managerial Power in Government, Business and Military organizations to reflect their population's proportion in the society; we will never have another Racial Problem in this Nation. Their positions alone will visually demonstrate to all members of the minority that we have 'Respect' for all members of all populations in our Nation.